TIME TRAVELERS

BOG
BODIES

Janet Buell

Twenty-First Century Books
A Division of Henry Holt and Company ~ New York

Twenty-First Century Books
A Division of Henry Holt and Company, Inc.
115 West 18th Street
New York, NY 10011

Henry Holt® and colophon are trademarks of
Henry Holt and Company, Inc.
Publishers since 1866

Published in Canada by Fitzhenry & Whiteside Ltd.
195 Allstate Parkway, Markham, Ontario, L3R 4T8

Library of Congress Cataloging-in-Publication Data
Buell, Janet.
Bog bodies / Janet Buell.
p.   cm.—(Time travelers)
Includes bibliographical references and index.
Summary: Focuses on the discovery of Lindow Man in England in 1984 while
also discussing other bog bodies and the information they reveal about
themselves, their manner of death, and the civilizations in which they lived.
1. Lindow Man—Juvenile literature. 2. Bog bodies—Juvenile literature.
[1. Bog bodies. 2. Lindow Man. 3. Human remains (Archaeology).
4. England—Antiquities.] I. Title. II. Series.
GN780.22.G7B84   1997
599.9—dc21

ISBN 0-8050-5164-3
First Edition—1997

Designed by Kelly Soong
Map by Jeffrey L. Ward

Printed in Mexico
All first editions are printed on acid-free paper ∞.

1 3 5 7 9 10 8 6 4 2

Photo Credits

Cover: © Archäologisches Landesmuseum der Christian-Albrechts-Universität, Schloss Gotorf, Germany;
p. 8: © Chief Constable of Cheshire; p. 10: © AP/Wide World Photos; p. 11: © Breck P. Kent/Earth
Scenes; p. 14: © Reg Davis; pp. 16, 29 (both), 31 (bottom): © British Museum; pp. 18, 31 (top): © The
Granger Collection; pp. 21, 42, 43: © Archäologisches Landesmuseum der Christian-Albrechts-
Universität, Schloss Gottorf, Germany; p. 23: © Forhistorisk Museum, Moesgård, Denmark; p. 25:
© Corbis-Bettmann; p. 25 (inset): © D. Cavagnaro/Visuals Unlimited; p. 35: © Collections/Brian
Shuel; p. 44 (both): © Malcolm Denemark; p. 47: © Rick Turner.

To Keith
for everything

ACKNOWLEDGMENTS

Many thanks to archaeologist Rick Turner of Cadw Welsh Historic Monuments. Thanks also to my editor Pat Culleton for her guidance.

CONTENTS

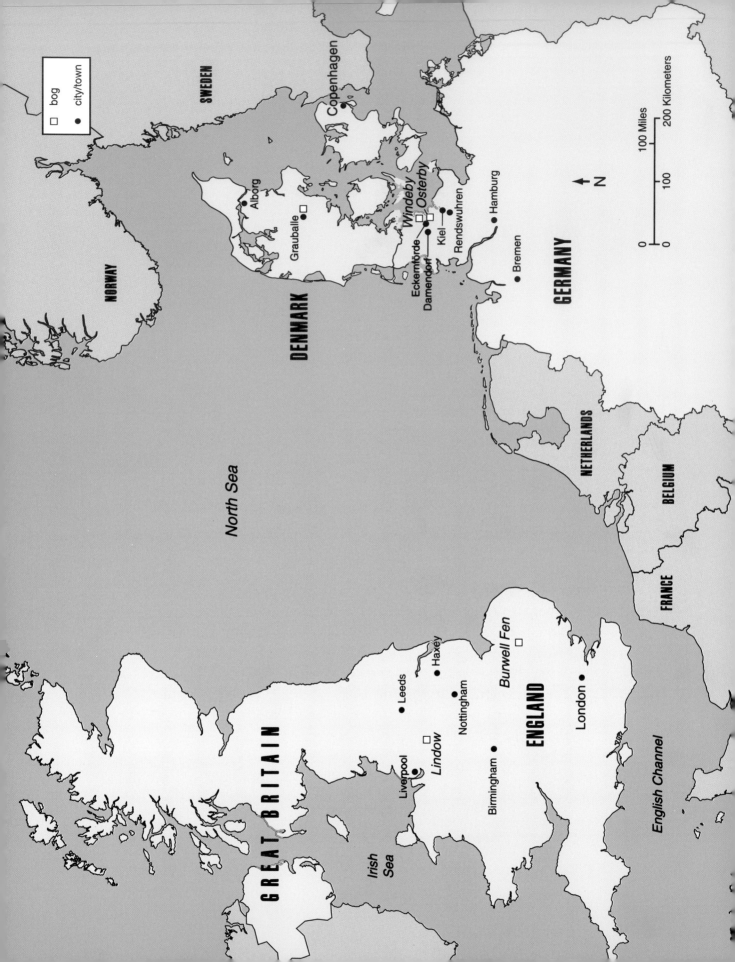

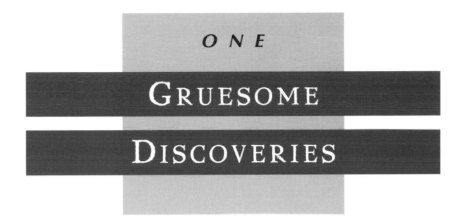

ONE

GRUESOME

DISCOVERIES

Soggy peat squished beneath archaeologist Rick Turner's boots as he scanned the cut bank of the peat bog. The English air hung damp and thick, and gray clouds covered the August sun. A steady drone from the harvesting machine mingled with sounds of traffic and chirping birds. On the far side of the bog, peatmen labored. The workers were finally back at their jobs, the memory of yesterday's events beginning to fade from their minds.

Maybe they haven't forgotten, thought Turner. A discovery like that is something that stays with you for life. He felt sure the peatworkers would tell their story again and again to children and friends, perhaps during deepest winter as night crept over Lindow bog.

As he searched, Turner considered the events that brought him to this boggy wetland. The previous afternoon, he had been busy in his office, writing reports on old churches. A reporter called to ask what he thought of the gruesome bog discovery. Turner wasn't sure. It was the first he'd heard of it.

Peatworker Andy Mould found the thing, the reporter told him. That wasn't too surprising. It was Mould's job to pick debris from the peat as it trundled by on the elevator belt. His sharp eyes kept rocks, sticks, and other things from fouling the teeth of the giant grinding machine.

Mould meant it as a joke when he plucked a peat-covered log from the conveyor belt and threw it at a co-worker. But when the log hit the ground, peat flew off it, revealing something more sinister than a mere joke. Though it was dark and shriveled, neither man doubted what lay before them.

It was a foot. A human foot.[1]

TWICE IN A LIFETIME

You would think making a gruesome find like that would be a once in a lifetime thing, but it was the second time for Andy Mould. A year earlier, in 1983, Mould pulled a round peat-covered object off the elevator belt at Lindow bog. He laughingly called it a dinosaur egg, but when he and co-workers cleaned it, they found it wasn't an egg at all. It was the upper half of a human skull. Patches of hair still stuck to its dome, and part of its left eyeball, though dark and shrunken, sat within its socket.

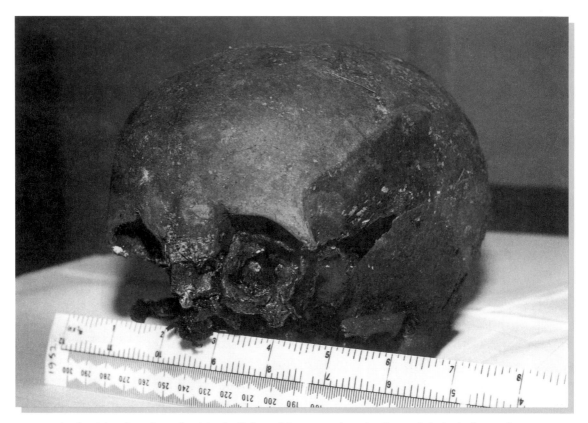

Authorities first thought this skull found in a peat bog in Great Britain belonged to a 1960 murder victim. Scientists later determined the skull was more than 1,500 years old.

When police saw the skull, they were sure they had finally solved the mysterious disappearance of a local woman who had vanished twenty-three years earlier. Police had always suspected that Peter Reyn-Bardt, the woman's husband, had murdered her, but without a body they couldn't prove it.[2]

Now, it appeared they had their proof. At the police lab, forensic anthropologists, the scientists who study human bones, found clues that pointed to the person's identity. They knew that the bone of a woman's skull tends to be thinner than a man's. A man's skull usually has a heavier supraorbital ridge, the part of the skull that runs beneath the eyebrows.[3] The skull's size and shape and lack of a heavy brow bone suggested it belonged to a woman between thirty and fifty years old. Mrs. Reyn-Bardt was thirty-five when she disappeared.[4] It appeared police had found at least part of the murdered woman's body.

Police questioned Peter Reyn-Bardt again. When they told him a woman's skull had been found in the bog, he broke down and confessed to the murder. Within a year, Reyn-Bardt was tried, convicted, and sentenced to prison.

As scientists continued to study the skull, they decided that it could not be Mrs. Reyn-Bardt's. It looked as if it had been in the bog much longer than the two decades Mrs. Reyn-Bardt had been missing.[5]

Nowadays, peat digging is a major industrial operation. Dried peat burns almost as well as coal and is used by many countries to fire the electric generators that provide energy to their people.

Peat is also dug on a smaller scale. Just like their ancestors before them, country folk throughout Europe and Great Britain still cut peat into blocks, then stack it to dry in the warm sun. In winter, they heat their homes and cook their fragrant winter stews by burning it in small peat stoves.

There was only one way scientists would know for sure. The evidence they needed would come from a test called carbon dating. Willard Libby invented the technique in 1947 and won the Nobel Prize for it in 1960. Carbon dating measures the age of living things and seawater, which contain a slightly radioactive substance called carbon 14 (C14). After the death of a living thing, C14 breaks down, or decays, at a particular rate, releasing its radioactivity. Scientists use that rate and the amount of C14 left in an object to tell how old it is.[6]

After weeks of testing, results showed the skull was more than fifteen hundred years old. It was not poor Mrs. Reyn-Bardt after all. It was an ancient woman, returned from her peaty grave to help police solve one of the community's most frustrating and puzzling crimes.

Willard Libby (right) *won the 1960 Nobel Prize for Chemistry for inventing the carbon-dating technique now widely used by forensic scientists.*

WEIRD BOGS

As weird as it might seem, most peatworkers don't consider it too unusual to have dead bodies lying around in their peat bogs, although it's *not* an everyday occurence. Over the last several centuries, peat diggers in Great Britain and Europe have found hundreds of them.

Sometimes these bog bodies are just a tangle of damp skin lying amid bits of cloth. Others are full bodies, still wearing their skin, eyelashes, and fingernails. Sometimes the body represents an accidental drowning or, as with the Reyn-Bardt case, a possible murder. Other times it's a body left over from the days when people killed criminals and buried them in the bog. Still others were given as human sacrifices by ancient Iron Age people who believed the offering would please their gods.[7]

In the early days of America, Native American women diapered their babies with sphagnum moss. Its hollow leaves make the plant very absorbent—a perfect substance for the job. During World War I, medical teams used sphagnum moss to dress soldiers' wounds. Besides being inexpensive, it also produces a natural antibiotic that helped the soldiers heal faster.

A typical bog in the Pine Barrens of New Jersey

A bog is a wetland area where things decay slowly. Canada has the most bogland, with 425 million acres. The former Soviet Union has 375 million acres. The United States is third with 75 million acres. Part of the unusual preserving powers of bogs has to do with water and the oxygen it holds. Most water regenerates its oxygen supply through movement. As it splashes over rocks, bubbles through crevices, and plunges over steep outcroppings, water collects the oxygen molecules it needs to support plant, fish, and microbe growth.

Unlike the water in rivers, lakes, and even swamps and marshes, bog water hardly moves. This stillness makes it a very oxygen-poor environment and a difficult place for decomposers to live. Without bacteria and other microbes, bog water becomes much like an airtight museum case, keeping treasures of the past away from organisms that normally break down human tissue, hair, and bone.

Bog water also preserves in the same way vinegar preserves pickles. Vinegar is an acid, which slows the action of decomposers. Bogs don't contain vinegar, but they are full of the humic acid released by plants. This acid controls other decomposers that can live in oxygen-poor water.[8]

The bogs that best preserve human bodies are the ones that contain sphagnum moss, which you may know as peat moss, a dried plant substance used in gardening. Like many other plants, sphagnum moss produces a chemical called tannin. Tannin is the same substance used to tan the skins and hides of animals for leather. Sphagnum moss produces a special kind of tannin that helps preserve human and animal flesh.[9]

MURDER IS ONE THING

To an archaeologist, recent murder is one thing—ancient murder is another. Until tests could be done on the foot, there was no way of knowing whom it belonged to. All Turner knew was that somewhere in Lindow bog there was likely to be a body that matched it.

The soggy landscape of Lindow bog stretches across hundreds of acres. Where would Turner begin? The foot had been found in peat harvested months earlier and then trucked to another site to dry. The manager could only point Turner to the vicinity where a body might lie. It wasn't much, but it was a start.

Farmers also use peatlands to grow crops such as timber, vegetables, and fruits, including the most famous bog product, cranberries. Bogs were also an early source of iron for the United States. Under certain conditions, the chemicals in a bog can react with one another to form a low-grade iron ore. This ore was a major source of iron until richer deposits of high-grade iron were discovered in Pennsylvania and Minnesota.

Turner searched for more than an hour before he found something that made his heart race. Before him, a flap of dark skin protruded from the cut edge of the bank. It was human skin, but Turner couldn't be sure how much of it lay embedded in the peat.

Police decided to let the archaeologist remove the body, if there was one, but they would give him only a day to do it. Already word of the discovery had spread through the area. Curiosity seekers were sure to descend on Lindow bog, and police feared they would make the investigation impossible.

Turner gathered a few scientist friends and police to help him dig out a block of peat surrounding the skin. When they finally freed it from the bog, they slid the block onto a plywood board. It took six men to hoist it onto a portable narrow-gauge railroad car used for hauling moss out of the bog.

Once on dry land, they loaded the peat into a van, which took it to the Macclesfield District General Hospital mortuary, where the dead are kept. It was here that the body would await results of carbon-dating tests. And it was here Rick Turner would face his toughest challenge yet.[10]

TWO

FORENSIC SCIENTISTS
MEET ANCIENT HUMAN

Since Mrs. Reyn-Bardt's disappearance, police looked forward to the day the bog would finally yield her body. Eager to begin their investigation, police pathologists hatched a plan to remove the corpse from the block of peat the next morning. It was the pathologists' job to determine when and how the bog person had died.

Turner knew that could mean archaeological disaster. If an ancient body lay within it, the surrounding moss might reveal valuable information. Preserved plant pollen could tell them the type of plants that grew in and around the bog when the body came to rest there. The plants could tell them about the climate at the time of the bog person's death. And it could help them determine the approximate year of death. In their eagerness to get to the body, the pathologists could accidentally destroy ancient evidence. Turner knew he would have to stop them.[1]

Early next morning, he and a fellow scientist arrived with the tools and materials they hoped would keep police from dismantling the block of peat: boards, nails, hammers, plastic wrap, and expanding polyurethane foam. Hurriedly, they pieced together a box from the boards. Then they wrapped the block of peat in plastic and placed it in the box. Finally, they sprayed plastic foam into the crevices, which expanded and hardened, then nailed a top onto the box. When the pathologists arrived, they found the mummy wrapped tightly in a new coffin. The archaeologist had thwarted their plans.

13

How frustrating a wait can be! Was there an ancient body in the block of peat or a modern one? Until scientists arrived to take samples of skin for the carbon-dating tests, waiting was all they could do.

Or was it? One pathologist had a clever idea. X-ray the block of peat, he suggested. An X ray would tell them if there was a body in it. Also, reasoned the scientists, most modern humans have some form of metal in or on their body, like dental fillings or jewelry. Metal would show up on an X ray.

Turner and his colleagues quickly wheeled the box to the X-ray lab. When the radiologist showed them the lab films, they could see a shadowy figure within the block. Though its lower half was missing, the curved skull and arched backbone were unmistakable. It was a human body. There were no dental fillings or other metal objects to be seen.

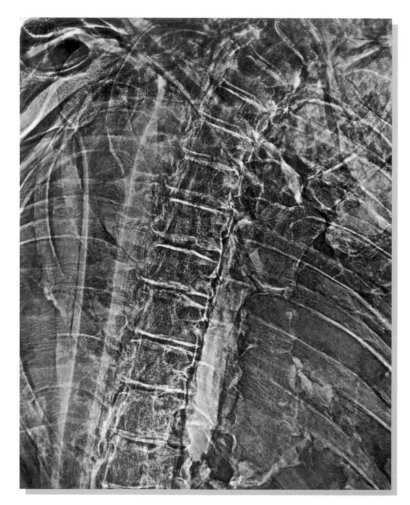

Scientists X-rayed the block of peat to see if it contained a body. The X rays clearly showed a human spinal column.

Finally, they knew for sure that a human lay within the peat. And it appeared to be very, very old—dating from at least A.D. 50, final tests would eventually reveal.[2] Denmark had its share of famous ancient bog people, and now it seemed England would have one, too.

ANCIENT TIME TRAVELER

News of the time traveler electrified the scientific community. Within a few days, the peat block sat in an examination room at the British Museum lab site called Franks House. Rick Turner returned to his work as county archaeologist, and now specialists from all over England gathered to exhume, or remove, the corpse from the mossy block.

The scientists knew they had to do whatever they could to preserve this echo of Great Britain's past. That would mean they would have to investigate carefully, removing peat and recording information as they went.

In their bid to save the bog mummy, the scientists confronted a major obstacle. With the help of bog preservatives, the body had survived for more than two thousand years. Now heat, humidity, and scavenging organisms threatened to undo all that work.

Molds, bacteria, and insects thrive in warm, moist temperatures. If left unchecked, they would eventually invade the surfaces of the mummy's skin. To keep invaders at bay, scientists placed the block of peat in a coffin cooler when they weren't examining it. Later, they would bring in a large refrigerator to do the job.

When the mummy was out of cold storage, the breath and body heat of living humans warmed the air-conditioned room. To keep it cool, scientists decided bystanders would have to leave, including the TV crew that was filming the investigation. They would allow them back occasionally, but only for brief visits. The film crew completed its work, using remote cameras and cold lights.[3]

MUMMY REVEALED

Examiners began their work at the flap of skin. They removed the moss using wooden and plastic tools and even their gloved hands, making notes and taking samples as they went. For removing peat closest to the body, they used soft brushes and water sprays. A dental vacuum sucked away excess water.

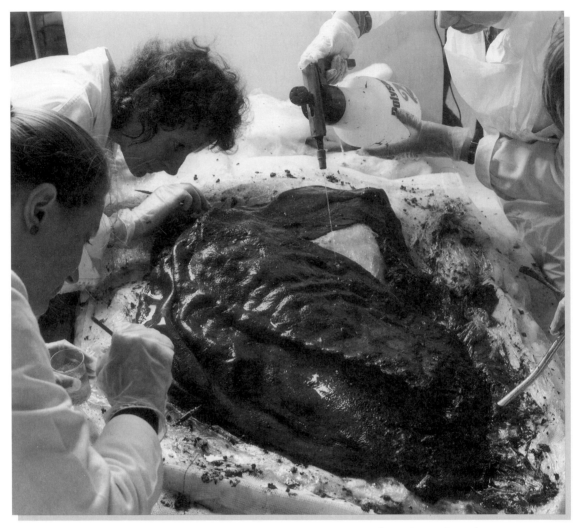

Scientists used distilled water to keep the skin moist as they cleaned Lindow man.

Slowly, a human form began to emerge. First to appear was the body's chest. Next was the left arm, which ended in a twist of flesh at the wrist. Three finger-nails—and a few finger bones—lay embedded in the peat where most of the hand had decayed. As scientists scraped away more of the moss, they discovered the body's outstretched and flattened right arm.

Finally, they uncovered the mummy's head. Its chin was pushed against its right shoulder at an awkward angle. Short brownish-red hair lay matted against its scalp, and a short beard covered its lower face. Until then, scientists hadn't known if the ancient human was male or female. Now they knew for sure, and they named him Lindow man for the bog that held him for so many centuries.

Lindow man seemed a flattened mess, but as he emerged from the peat, scientists couldn't help thinking how perfect he was. Centuries in the bog had turned his skin to soft, dark leather. His powerful build told scientists that he had been a strong man. Even in death Lindow man looked healthy and well nourished. The scientists imagined him alive, the muscles rippling smoothly as he moved.

As each layer of peat came away, scientists grew more curious about the ancient bog man. The date of death meant he was likely a Celt, one of the ancient people who once inhabited Great Britain. But why had this Celtic man been buried in the bog so many centuries ago? Had he drowned? Was he a criminal? Or was he the victim of human sacrifice?[4]

Depending on the climate, different regions of the world have different types of peat. Sedges and heaths populate the bogs of Ireland, Great Britain, and some European countries. These plants make a peat that burns easily. Russian scientists have developed many products from peat: medicines, animal feed, polishes, pesticides, building material, and products to clean up oil spills, for example.

A CASE OF OVERKILL

Where would you start searching for clues to death? If you are a medical examiner, you start with the autopsy. *Autopsy* comes from a Greek word that means "to see with your own eyes." During an autopsy, doctors and other scientists examine the inside and outside of a dead body.

As the peat came away from the corpse, examiners could see that Lindow man's last moments had been violent ones. At the top of his head, two jagged gashes split the skin. Another injury had opened skin at the back of his skull.

At first scientists believed the gashes might have been caused postmortem, which is Latin for "after death." Centuries in the bog could have caused these tears in the bog man's once-fragile skin. But as they examined the wounds more closely, they could see what looked like bits of shattered bone lying beneath the cuts. X rays of his skull confirmed that fragments of scalp bone had lodged deep within Lindow man's head.

When scientists magnified the wounds through a microscope, they could see their edges had torn in a particular way. Those tears looked like the kind a small, narrow-edged ax would make. The depth of the wounds' edges showed that the blows could only have come from above and behind, which meant Lindow man

17

was probably kneeling when someone struck him. The skin around the injuries had swelled from blood flowing to it, so Lindow man had been alive, though probably unconscious, after someone delivered the terrible ax blows.

Another ominous clue surfaced as scientists continued their investigation. Circling Lindow man's neck was what at first appeared to be a root from a bog plant. Looking closely, they discovered it wasn't a root at all but a thin, knotted cord biting deeply into the mummy's neck. Scientists knew the Celts wore decorative necklaces called torcs, but this appeared bound too tightly to be a decoration. The cord looked tight enough to strangle.

The scientists had taken detailed pictures of Lindow man's insides with the help of a CAT scanner. CAT is short for computed axial tomography. Unlike a reg-

Celts often wore torcs, which were necklaces of bronze or gold. Scientists first thought Lindow man was wearing a torc but later realized he had been strangled with a cord.

ular X-ray machine, a CAT scan helps scientists and doctors visualize a more detailed picture of a body's interior by taking X rays of the body in thin slices. A computer then takes these X rays and changes them into three-dimensional images, allowing scientists a better view of the body's internal structures without having to cut it open.[5]

The CAT scans showed fractures in the two neck vertebrae beneath the knotted cord. Putting these clues together, scientists realized that someone had garroted Lindow man. Garroting is a form of strangulation performed by inserting a stick into a neck noose and giving it a quick twist. In this case, it broke Lindow man's neck, too.

The scalp wounds and strangle cord were enough to kill Lindow man, but investigators found more. He suffered rib fractures that were likely caused by a heavy blow to his back. And as they lifted his head, they found a puncture wound in Lindow man's neck. The wound had cut through the man's jugular vein, a main blood vessel to the head.[6]

What did all this violence mean? Why were there so many wounds? Any one of them may have been enough to kill Lindow man. The bog man's death was beginning to look like more than a simple case of murder.

THREE

DEAD MEN

DO TELL TALES

In the 1600s, poet John Dryden wrote that "dead men tell no tales."[1] But Dryden never met a bog man . . . or a modern scientist. If he had, he would have known the dead *do* speak. Their voices may be silent, yet their bodies—when we discover them and know how to look at them—still whisper ancient secrets to us.

Lindow man had a tale to tell, and scientists could help him tell it. They already knew he died a violent death. Now they would search for the details of that death and for clues to how he lived.

X rays and CAT scans of the bog man's bones already told scientists that Lindow man had been a healthy man and had died between the ages of twenty-five and thirty. The next step was to examine the rest of the mummy—its skin, organs, hair, and nails—with the same tools doctors use to diagnose diseases.

HAIR-RAISING TALES FROM THE GRAVE

Hair is tough stuff. It contains keratin, a protein made of strong fibers that don't dissolve easily in water. Keratin makes up the outer layers of horn, hair, feathers, hoofs, nails, claws, and bills. It's so tough that artifacts made of these things can last for hundreds or even thousands of years. Keratin is an archaeologist's dream come true.[2]

20

A head found in Germany is just one example of keratin's amazing staying power. Whoever beheaded the ancient man buried his head in Osterby bog. There, the skin disintegrated until only a skull remained, which was topped by a full head of hair. That hair, which is about a foot long, had been gathered on one side and then twisted into an ingenious knot that, to this day, stays in place without hairpins.

Tacitus was a Roman who described Germans at the end of the first century A.D. He wrote that a tribe called the Swabians knotted their hair as Osterby man did. Scientists call Osterby man's hairdo a "Swabian knot" after his ancient people.[3]

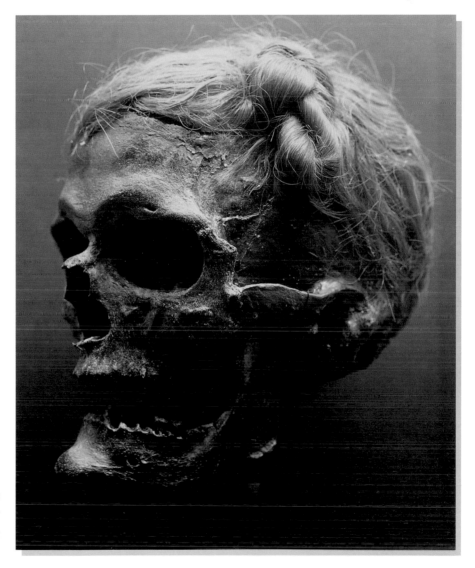

This skull has its original hair twisted into a Swabian knot.

21

Celtic men didn't wear Swabian knots, but they often wore beards. Lindow man was no exception. The Italian writer Diodorus Siculus said this about the Celts: "Some of them shave the beard, but others let it grow a little; and the nobles shave their cheeks, but they let the moustache grow until it covers the mouth. Consequently, when they are eating, their moustaches become entangled in the food, and when they are drinking, the beverage passes, as it were, through a kind of strainer."[4]

Though the peat had stained it a brownish-red, the bog man's hair was in fine shape after its long burial. It was so well preserved that scientists could see how badly it had been trimmed. The very tips of the hair looked jagged, too.

The scientists decided to compare the bog man's hair against modern hair that had been cut with a razor and a scissors. Under the scanning electron microscope (SEM), which can reveal things as small as an atom, they could see that Lindow man's hair didn't have the smooth, angled surface of a razor cut. The ends had a "stepped" look that matched the modern hairstyle cut with a scissors. It was clear he had used one to trim his beard.

While it may seem unimportant that Lindow man used scissors, scientists learned a lot from this fact. Archaeologists say that scissors weren't used in Great Britain until after the first century A.D., when Romans invaded. A rare tool like a pair of scissors wasn't available to just any Celtic person. It meant that Lindow man was likely high ranking in his tribe, a man privileged enough to use this new technology brought by the Romans.[5]

ANOTHER TALE TO TELL

Scientists could see how nicely trimmed and well shaped Lindow man's nails appeared to be. They decided to do another study with the SEM, this time comparing them with the nails of four different people. For comparison, they chose a modern housewife, a teacher, a farmworker, and a medieval Irish bog woman.

Under the SEM, the edges and surfaces of Lindow man's nails looked smooth and clear. Like the teacher's and housewife's nails, Lindow man's were free from the gouges and scratches of rough outdoor work. Compared to the farmworker's nails with their deep scratches, Lindow man's looked as though he hadn't done a day of hard labor. The Irish bog woman had chipped and rough-looking nails, which told scientists that she, too, had used her hands for hard work. Lindow man's nails, like the scissors evidence, again pointed to his high status among his people.[6]

Though Lindow man's nails survived the centuries, his hands had not. They decayed in the peaty waters, leaving only a few soft finger bones. If they had survived, they may have told a story much like another mummy's hands do.

In 1952, peat diggers discovered a body in a little bog near Grauballe, Denmark. The Danish Iron Age man suffered a violent death about two thousand years ago. Other evidence showed that most likely his people sacrificed him to their gods. His throat had been cut, and his head had been bashed with a blunt-edged instrument.

The scientists who studied Grauballe man asked police fingerprint experts to look at the bog man's hands. It was the first time these scientists had seen the hands of a prehistoric bog body. At first, the criminologists couldn't believe Grauballe man was as old as scientists claimed. The curves and whorls of his fingerprints were clearer than their own. After analyzing the man's prints, the sci-

The hand of 2,000-year-old Grauballe man was so
well preserved even the fingerprints were clearly visible.

A SEM is a very powerful tool scientists use to look at bacteria, viruses, and other things. It works by first creating an electron beam that's focused through a series of electrical fields. The highly focused beam is then aimed at the object, which has been coated with vaporized gold, used to conduct electricity. When it strikes, it causes the object's surface to emit a different type of electron. These electrons are then translated into a signal. The signals are then changed into an image of the surface. The Lindow-man scientists used the beam to magnify the surface of the bog man's hairs to three hundred times their normal size.

entists discovered that fingerprints haven't changed at all in two thousand years. They match the same patterns common in Denmark today.

Grauballe man's hands looked as if he had never done a lick of rough work. Like Lindow man, the Grauballe bog man was probably a high-ranking person within his tribe.[7]

A GUT FEELING

A peat bog can be unpredictable when it comes to what is and what is not preserved in it. Grauballe man's hands survived burial. Lindow man's hands did not. One bog person, Tollund man, unearthed by Danish peat diggers in 1950, looks as though he has just nodded off for a short nap. In fact, he died two thousand years ago. Another bog body, the Damendorf man of Germany, didn't fare as well. While his hair, shoes, and leather belt lasted through a two-thousand-year bog burial, the body is only an empty sack of skin.

One thing that usually survives a bog burial is what scientists call the gut—a person's esophagus, stomach, and intestines. Other organs may dissolve in acidic peat water, but the gut is made to withstand strong digestive acids.[8] This is a real boon to phytoarchaeologists, who learn about the past by studying the things people ate. These plant archaeologists usually investigate the campfires and storage pits ancient people left behind. They even investigate the fossilized remains they find in prehistoric toilets. And sometimes they have to pick through the gut contents of dead people.

The first step phytoarchaeologists take is to separate the particles of undigested or partially digested food. For example, they look at cereal grains and wild plants with a microscope and compare them to other grains. They can tell by the shape of those grains whether they came from a barley plant, a wheat plant, or a weed plant. This evidence tells the archaeologists what plants and crops ancient people grew.

The phytoarchaeologists also look for fruits or vegetables the person may have swallowed. These can pinpoint the time of year a person died. Sloeberries found in the stomach of the five-thousand-year-old Ice Man tell scientists that the prehistoric hunter probably died in the autumn. That's when sloeberries ripen.[9]

THE LAST MEAL

Would Lindow man's gut tell a similar tale? His lower intestines were gone, hacked off in the bog by the giant peat excavator, but he still had his stomach and small intestines. This part of his gut held the remains of a small meal. There was no evidence of fresh fruits or vegetables, so scientists can't tell what time of year he died.

Druids thought mistletoe (inset) was a sacred plant and collected it for use in their rituals.

Phytoarchaeologists discovered a mix of grains in the bog man's stomach. Tests show that the grain had been heated to a temperature for making flatbread. Surprisingly, that small bit of bread was burned, which as you will see later may have had something to do with the man's death.

Along with the burned bread, scientists found mistletoe pollen. Mistletoe is a parasitic plant that grows and feeds on trees. Some scientists believe the presence of this pollen is evidence that Lindow man may have been a human sacrifice. The ancient Greek and Roman historians wrote that Celts considered mistletoe a sacred plant. They used it as an antidote to poison and to keep their cattle fertile.[10]

The Celts had more deadly uses for the plant, too. The Roman naturalist Pliny and others wrote about how the Celtic priests, called Druids, used mistletoe in their religious ceremonies. Pliny wrote this about the Druids' rituals: "the Druids—for so their magicians are called—held nothing more sacred than the mistletoe and the tree that bears it, always supposing that tree to be the oak. . . . Clad in a white robe, the priest ascends the tree and cuts the mistletoe with a golden sickle, and it is received by others in a white cloak." Pliny goes on to say that the Druids then sacrificed a victim to please the Celtic gods.[11]

The scientists were gradually uncovering the buried pieces of the bog man's story. But it wasn't complete just yet. To fit these puzzle pieces together, they would have to look even deeper into the past.

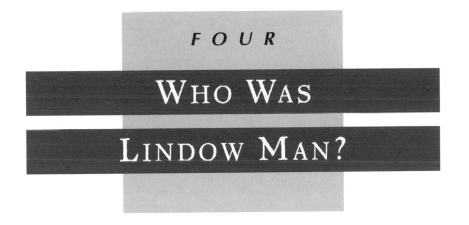

FOUR

WHO WAS

LINDOW MAN?

So what did the puzzle pieces tell scientists about Lindow man? They knew he was a powerfully built, healthy Celtic man. He was brutally killed and buried in Lindow bog. His well-manicured nails show he wasn't a farmer or slave but a high-ranking person. He was privileged enough to trim his beard with scissors. The mistletoe pollen in his gut links him with the mysterious Celtic priests called Druids.[1]

Technology helps us construct a picture of Lindow man's life, but it doesn't show us the whole picture. To find out more, we have to become time travelers ourselves and return to the days of the bog man's people, to the Celts of early Great Britain. For the journey we need the road maps called archaeology and history. Together, they give us a fine view of the Celts, even though they are thousands of years away from us.

Archaeologists are the scientists who interpret the lives of ancient people by looking at the things they left behind. The artifacts and other evidence found in Celtic burial sites and in the ruins of their villages tell us a lot about the way the Lindow man's people lived.

Unlike archaeology, history relies on written language. Unfortunately, the Celts didn't record their history on paper or stone. Instead, they memorized their tales, legends, and songs, and passed these orally from one generation to the next.[2]

Still, we can know the Celts because of what others wrote about them. These people were the Romans and Greeks, whom we call the classical writers. These historians came to know the Celts through war and trading contacts.

The classical writers and Celts were as different as two groups of people can be. Though Greeks and Romans admired Celtic courage, they found Celtic behavior barbaric, especially their practice of head hunting and human sacrifice. Since they wrote with such a prejudiced view, we can't always trust the accuracy of classical accounts. Despite this, there is enough truth in their words, and in the archaeological record, to give us a good idea of Celtic life.[3]

ANCIENT ORIGINS

The origins of Lindow man's people are a mystery, but we know that by twenty-five centuries ago, they had settled throughout Europe and Great Britain. The Celts of Great Britain, who are often called Britons, didn't rely on a central government. Instead, their society was made up of individual chiefdoms, ruled by a chieftain or king.

As in many societies, several classes of people lived and worked within each chiefdom. The lowest of these were freemen. The highest ranking Celts belonged to the warrior class and to people of art, such as Druids, lawyers, craftsmen, and doctors.

The Britons were family people, too. Unlike our small families, as many as four generations lived together in the same large house—children, cousins, parents, aunts and uncles, grandparents, and often, great-grandparents—as many as twenty to thirty people. Most Celts made their living by raising wheat, barley, sheep, cattle, and pigs.[4]

BRAGGARTS AND PEACOCKS

The classical writers tell us Celtic men and women were tall and handsome, with pale skin and light hair. They took great pride in their appearance and boldly ornamented themselves with jewelry and other finery. Diodorus Siculus wrote that they "amass a great amount of gold, which is used for ornament not only by the women but also by the men. For around their wrists and arms they wear bracelets, around their necks heavy necklaces of solid gold, and huge rings they wear as well."

Burial excavations show the astonishing artistic skills of their metalworkers. Beautifully worked brooches, enameled armbands, bronze bracelets, torcs of gold,

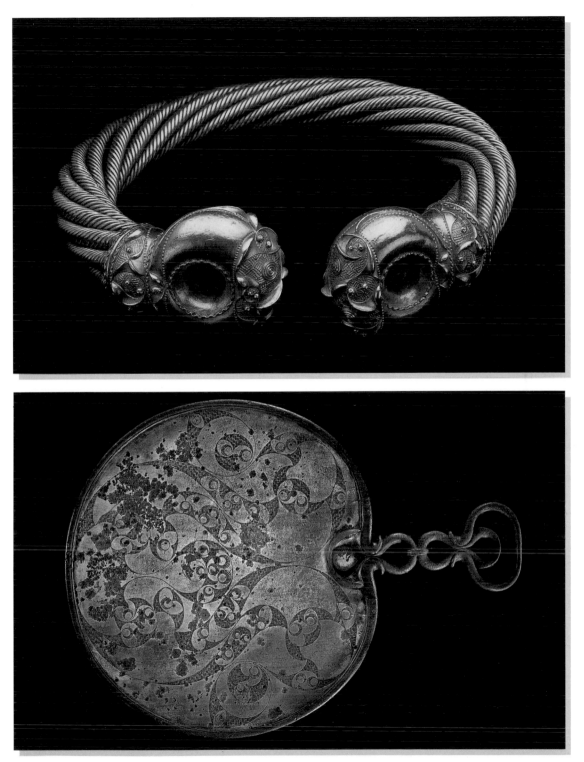

An elaborate Celtic torc of gold (top) *and a decorated mirror* (bottom)

and other necklaces made of coral or amber or glass beads fill the graves of their nobles.

Strabo, the Greek historian, tells us that the Celts were so proud of their appearance that they punished any man in their tribe whose belly grew large from too much food and drink. The Celtic pride also showed in the clothing they wore.

Siculus wrote that the the ancient Britons favored striking clothing, "shirts which have been dyed and embroidered in various colors, and breeches . . . and they wear striped cloaks, fastened by a brooch on the shoulder." The Romans, who wore a sheetlike outfit called a toga, considered Celtic "breeches," or pants, unmanly.

The Celts had a reputation of being braggarts, and all this finery was just one more way of "boasting" about themselves. Another way was to give lavish gifts to friends and loyal followers. Nobles hired accomplished poets and musicians, called bards, to tell everyone of their kind, generous, and courageous deeds.[5]

THE FIERCE AND TERRIBLE CELTS

"The whole race . . . is war-mad, and both high-spirited and quick for battle, although otherwise simple and not ill-mannered." This is what Strabo, a Greek historian, wrote about the Celts. He wasn't alone in his thinking. There were many who viewed the Celts as an aggressive and "war-mad" people.

This reputation was justified. The Celts became legendary for their wild war tactics. Many of them fought with vengeance to the death. Some Celts went into battle naked, probably to show their great courage by going "unarmored" into war or for some religious reason that's lost to us now.

The Celts had plenty of opportunity to make war. Territorial disputes, interfamily feuds, and cattle raids were just some of the reasons Celts fought. Some Celts made war a career, but most didn't. While the warriors were off fighting, daily life usually continued peacefully.[6]

The head was so important to the Celts that they often took the heads of their fallen enemies, most likely to control the spirit that dwelled within them. Diodorus Siculus wrote that "When their enemies fall, they cut off their heads and fasten them about the necks of their horses. . . and these first-fruits of battle they fasten by nails upon their houses. . . . The heads of their most distinguished enemies they embalm in cedar-oil and carefully preserve in a chest, and these they exhibit to strangers."

These ancient items of war are a Celtic bronze-and-gold helmet (above) *from the third century* B.C. *and a Celtic shield* (right).

31

The Spiritual Celts

Running beneath the artistic and fighting nature of the Celts was a spiritual side. The scientists who studied Lindow man believed that Celtic religious beliefs could help them understand his violent death.

The Celts believed in many gods. The word *pagan* is used to describe this kind of belief. The Celtic gods lived within natural things like trees, water, and hills. The Celts believed that keeping their gods happy would mean that no disasters would befall them. With the gods' help, they would have good weather. With the gods' help, they would have a plentiful harvest. With the gods' help, they would be victorious in battle.

The Celts celebrated and honored their gods with many yearly holidays. The two most important were Samain and Beltain.

In the spring, the Celts honored their god Belenos during a festival they called Beltain. During Beltain festivities, two giant bonfires burned on a hilltop. The Celts drove their cattle between them to "cleanse" them of evil spirits before they let them out to graze. As with all Celtic holidays, Druids presided over the Beltain celebrations.

Samain, on the eve of November 1, celebrated the end of one year and the beginning of a new one. The Celts believed that during Samain the door between the real world and spiritual world opened. In the darkening days of autumn, goblins and ghosties and bogeymen were afoot. Today, some people celebrate what remains of this grim Celtic holiday, which we now call Halloween.[7]

A Sacrificial Victim?

To keep them happy, Celtic people offered their gods presents, called sacrifices. They placed these offerings in special places, particularly in water, which the Celts viewed as most sacred. Spectacular examples of those sacrifices turn up in bogs, wells, streams, and rivers wherever Celtic people lived. Fabulous torcs, rings, armbands, goblets, weapons of war, chariots, and other fancy carts are just some of these offerings. Often, the objects have been "killed," that is, broken or bent in some way.

Beautiful objects weren't the only thing Celtic people sacrificed for their gods. Some-

> The most common human sacrifices unearthed in Great Britain are human heads. Lindow woman, the first Lindow bog discovery, was likely one of those sacrifices.

times, they offered animals such as dogs or cattle, especially white bulls. Occasionally, they offered human lives, which they considered their most precious gift.

While human sacrifice may seem as horrible to us as it did to the classical writers, it was a natural part of Celtic spiritual beliefs. They strongly believed that a glorious life awaited them after they died. This may explain why they were such courageous fighters. The sacrificial victims may have been considered messengers to the gods, and may have gone willingly to their death, considering it an honor to be chosen for the job.[8]

Was Lindow man a sacrificial victim? Although scientists can't be completely sure, there is strong evidence that suggests he was. The bog man was obviously a high-ranking Celt, an offering the gods would have especially liked. His injuries show that his death wasn't a simple murder, but an elaborate execution. The wound in the bog man's neck could have been used to drain blood from his body, which the classical writers say was often part of the sacrificial ritual.

Lindow man's death happened two thousand years ago, at a time when Celts were known to make human sacrifices. His killers put his body in a bog, a watery place considered sacred by his people. Perhaps most tantalizing is the mistletoe pollen, conjuring up visions of the mystical Druids and their ancient, gruesome ceremonies.[9]

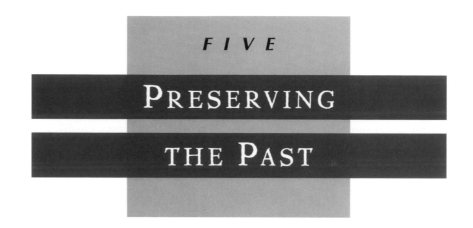

FIVE

PRESERVING THE PAST

We think human sacrifice is a terrible idea, so it's easy to believe the Celts were terrible people for the things they did. But the Celts weren't terrible people. They just didn't have the scientific knowledge we do to explain the natural world. The Celtic belief in human sacrifice began to change after the Romans invaded Celtic lands. The invasions started with Emperor Julius Caesar in 55 B.C. and continued sporadically until A.D. 43, when Emperor Claudius finally conquered the Celts.

The Romans wanted the Celts to obey them, so they allowed the Celts to keep some of their religious practices but passed laws making it illegal for the Druids to preside over Celtic ceremonies. They also outlawed human sacrifice. But the Celts believed strongly in their gods, and many still practiced their religion secretly.

Eventually, Germanic tribes called the Angles and Saxons, who later became known as the English, moved into Great Britain. Soon, the Romans lost their hold on Celtic lands. During this time, a new religion was spreading throughout Europe. People called this new religion Christianity. When it finally reached Celtic lands, the old ways began to change forever.[1]

WHO WILL BE OUR GOD?

The change to Christianity was a gradual one. As time passed, the Celts embraced the new message of peace and brotherhood. Still, the old superstitions lingered.

The Celts found it wasn't simple to change allegiance from one god to another. Many still felt uneasy to abandon their old gods. They continued to celebrate the old ceremonies and rituals.

To make it easier for Celts, the priests took their pagan beliefs and gave them a Christian slant. The Celtic goddess Brigid, whose reign was celebrated on February 1, became the Christian saint of the same name. Samain became the church holiday called All Hollows' Eve. All Saints' Day is celebrated immediately afterward, on November 1.[2]

Even now, at least some of the old Celtic ceremonies continue, though their pagan meaning is largely forgotten. For example, Well-Dressing still takes place in some parts of Great Britain. Typically, on a certain day in spring or summer, villagers decorate the town well with garlands of fruits, vegetables, and other summer greenery. Some well-dressing decorations are very elaborate. Where there are no town wells, the people decorate community water spigots. These well-dressing rituals date back to the days when Celts believed some of their gods lived in water.

Villagers in Tissington, England, prepare an elaborate Well-Dressing of flower petals, grasses, and other natural substances.

The Celts continued to honor these watery places even after church leaders outlawed it. Eventually, the church gave in to the strength of old traditions. They spiritually "cleansed" the wells of their pagan gods and rededicated them to the Virgin Mary or to one of the Christian saints.

Few other rituals have survived into modern times. Many people are unhappy to see these ancient customs disappear, though no one is sorry to see an end to human sacrifice.

Fortunately, some people have thought it important enough to keep a record of these customs. Folklorists are people who collect and record such customs.[3] Folklore is the traditional beliefs, legends, and customs of a particular human culture, or folk.

In reading about these old ceremonies and customs, we sometimes find the pagan meaning within. We also find threads of evidence that lead us to the rituals surrounding Lindow man's last hours on earth.

> The Celts most especially honored the human head, where they believed the soul dwelled. Some anthropologists believe soccer was originally played with a human head, most likely that of a captured enemy. Even today, some Celtic descendants believe the cure for epilepsy is to drink water from a special well, using a cup made from the skull of one of their ancestors.

THE BLACKENED BREAD

Lindow man's last meal contained a burned portion of flat bread. This bread may be an echo of a long-ago ritual performed on May 1, during Beltain ceremonies. A folklorist named Martin Martin, who lived in the eighteenth century, wrote about one blackened bread ritual he witnessed in Scotland.

For this Beltain festival, celebrants baked a special thin cake, called a bannock, and made sure that one part of it was thoroughly burned. The bannock was then broken up and distributed among the villagers. The one who received the blackened part was called the "devoted."

After eating the blackened bit of cake, the devoted had to leap three times through the dying bonfire or was seized by the villagers, who pretended to throw the victim into the fire. Till the end of the festivities, villagers then referred to that person as "the dead."

Folklorists have recorded many instances of blackened bread ceremonies throughout Great Britain, and it has its roots in long-forgotten Celtic ceremonies. They believe that during ancient Beltain festivals, villagers really did devote one of their own to the gods. Throwing the victim into the fire was one way these ancient Britons sent the devoted into the afterlife.

As Celtic ways changed, people moved away from human sacrifice and eventually forgot the original meaning of this custom. The ceremony continued but became only a symbol of that sacrifice.

Could Lindow man have received the blackened bread during some ancient Beltain festival? Could he have been one of the devoted? We may never know for sure, but looking at the past through the eyes of science makes it an interesting possibility to consider.[4]

SMOKING THE FOOL

Another celebration, called the Haxey Hood Game, has its roots in very ancient rituals. The game still takes place today at the town of Haxey, on the Isle of Axholme in England. Villagers enact the Haxey Hood ritual every January 6, during the heart of midwinter.

Twelve Boggans, the King Boggan, and a Fool preside over the ceremonies. At 3 P.M., the Fool stands on a stone at the center of the village, where he makes a speech to the crowd. Near the end of this speech, the Boggans "smoke the Fool" by starting a fire at the man's feet. As smoke rises around him, the Fool ends his speech by saying:

> *Hoose agen hoose [house against house],*
> *toone agen toone [town against town],*
> *if thou meets a man, knock him down,*
> *but don't hurt him.*

Later, the Fool leads the way to a nearby field. With him go the Boggans, the villagers, and the King Boggan, who carries a long wand made of thirteen willow sticks bound together thirteen times. Then the battle for the Sway Hood begins.

The Sway Hood, which may have been a hood or hat in olden days, is now a thick, leather-bound rope, about two feet long. When the King Boggan throws the Sway Hood into the air, rival teams from around the island try to grab it and take it to one of three inns that serve as goals.

The teams use any means they can to win the Sway Hood, but they may not kick or toss it forward. Instead, the Hood is pushed, pulled, and dragged toward the goal. As it moves, the mob of players sways over the land, knocking down hedges and stone walls as it goes. The game can last for several hours and some-times people get hurt from the rough play.[5]

On the face of it, the Haxey Hood Game is nothing more than a strange game, but if you look closer, you can see echoes of an ancient Celtic ritual. The Boggans are a clear link to bogs. In fact, a boggan is just one of the names given to the spir-its believed by some people to walk there.

The celebration takes place near an area that has produced the largest number of sacrificial bog burials in Great Britain. Many of the bog bodies found through-out Europe and Great Britain wore hoods over their heads. Many had sticks buried beside them. These sticks remind some historians of the sticks the King Boggan carries during the opening ceremonies. Even the Sway Hood, a twisted rope, re-sembles the twisted ropes found around the necks of some bog burials and the torcs worn by the Celts.[6]

•　　•　　•

As you have seen, science and history allows us a glimpse into the past. But how can we know if our interpretation of these clues is accurate? The truth is, we can't. We weren't there ourselves, so we have to rely on the pictures created from an-cient puzzle pieces. Like the game of telephone, where one person starts a secret and passes it on to the next and so on, the original message changes. The same thing happens in human history.

Sometimes we never really understand the puz-zle pieces we find. Or we don't find enough of them to complete the picture. Fortunately for us, more of those puzzle pieces surface every year. Archaeolo-gists excavate ruined villages. Legends and customs are interpreted in new ways. And occasionally, an-other bog body presents itself, challenging us to un-lock the secrets of its past.

Lindow man wasn't com-pletely preserved after his long stay in the bog. Sci-entists decided to freeze-dry him to complete the process.

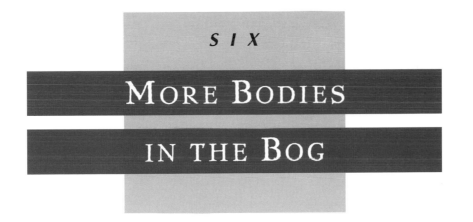

MORE BODIES
IN THE BOG

A bog is a strange and wonderful place, a land of weird plants, ancient legends, and of course, bog bodies. You may have never seen a bog, but they are far more common than you think. More than two million square miles of peat bog grow in all regions of the world except in Antarctica.

Bogs have always inspired legends and strange beliefs, perhaps because of ancient corpses that appear from their black depths. Some beliefs center around trolls and other spirits who are reported to walk the bog nightly. The word *bogeyman* comes from these legends. Sherlock Holmes fought a bog beast in the chilling tale *The Hound of the Baskervilles*. Even Shakespeare in his play *The Tempest* wrote, "All the infections that the sun sucks up / From bogs, fens, flats, on Prosper fall and make him / By inchmeal a disease!"[1]

The Celts weren't the only ones responsible for bodies in the bog. They come to us from many time periods and all parts of the globe. Sometimes these burials were purposeful. Other times death was accidental.

CAUGHT DEAD IN THE BOG

Bogs are notorious for their soggy, treacherous surfaces. A bog may quickly suck down an unlucky traveler who strays into its dark mire. One such bog body gives us a glimpse of this tragic life-and-death struggle. When found, the man lay face down, clutching tufts of bog heather in his hands as if to pull himself out of his trap.

Perhaps strangest of all discoveries are the heads and other body parts found in the dark quagmire. Lindow woman and the Swabian man were just two of many heads found in bogs.

In the early 1800s German peat diggers discovered a two-thousand-year-old leg still wearing its leather shoe. In another German bog, grave diggers in 1848 found two complete bodies riddled with arrowheads. With them lay four arms and two legs belonging to several different people. Though we do not know for certain, they were most likely the discarded amputations from a nearby medieval military field hospital. The bodies appear to be those of soldiers killed in battle.

Some bog bodies are even more gruesome. One German bog man who had been scalped clutched his severed ears and lips in his hands. We can only wonder what he did to deserve such a cruel punishment.

A number of bog burials were the result of superstitions of the time. Denied access to the holy ground of a cemetery, suicide victims often were buried in bogs. In the eleventh century, many believed that women who died in childbirth would drag their living child with them into the grave, so they buried the women in a bog instead.

Given how strange it is to find a bog body, it's not surprising their discovery aroused superstition and

There are so many naked bog bodies found it's easy to believe that many of them went to their graves clad only in their birthday suits. That's not necessarily true. Vegetable-based clothing like cotton or flax rarely survives the acidic waters of a peat bog. Despite the keratin found in animal hair, some garments made of it still disintegrate. When clothing does survive, it gives us a terrific view of the past. Finding a clothed bog body can help archaeologists learn such things as weaving techniques ancient people used and can pinpoint the age of the bog burial.

One such bog body is Huldre Fen woman, found in Denmark in 1879 during peat cutting. Huldre Fen woman was unusual in that she wore the most complete set of Iron Age clothing ever found.

Around her shoulders she wore two lambskin capes. A checked skirt circled her waist, fastened with a leather strap. She fastened her scarf with a bird bone pin. Her small purse, made of an animal bladder, contained a woolen hairband and another leather strap. In the pocket of her skirt was a beautifully carved wooden comb.

fear. Some people in the 1600s and 1700s considered them to be the work of the devil or other evil spirits. When bodies appeared from beneath the bog, frightened townspeople usually reburied them on the spot or carted them to a cemetery for a more proper burial.

Fortunately, there are some early accounts of bog bodies. The people who recorded them recognized that the bodies were not spirits to be feared. They knew these unfortunate victims were human and a tantalizing reminder of days long past.[2]

EARLIEST WRITTEN ACCOUNT

The earliest written account of bog bodies comes from Denmark in 1773. Peat diggers called a local judge when they found a body in the bog. After inspecting it, the judge declared that the body had been there for a very long time. He described the ancient human for readers of the local newspaper:

> The body lay stretched on its back with both arms crossed behind the back as if they had been tied together, although there was no trace of bindings. The body was entirely naked except for the head, which was encased in a sheepskin cape, on the removal of which it could be clearly seen that the man had a reddish beard and very short hair.[3]

The body lay beneath a network of branches and twigs. The judge believed the man's killers placed them there to keep the corpse from floating.

Although practicality might have been a reason for pinning down a bog body, being superstitious was often another. A heavy stone on the body or an anchored cage of willow branches might have given the killers some comfort. Pinned down like that, it was unlikely the victim's spirit would walk after death.

One bog woman's killers had exacted just such a cruel punishment. Her knee had swelled beneath the branched wooden stakes used to pin her to the bog. This meant she was alive when she had been trapped in the bog. Thousands of years later, her face still wore the look of despair you would expect from someone who had died such a horrible death.[4]

> Raised bogs can grow so high that they'll suddenly shift. A compact raised bog can move several miles, sometimes carrying bog bodies along, and end up covering many acres. Like an avalanche, it buries everything in its path.

CRIME AND PUNISHMENT

The Roman historian Tacitus wrote that prehistoric Germanic people punished their criminals in certain ways: "Traitors and deserters are hung from trees; cowards, poor fighters, and notorious evil-doers are plunged in the mud of marshes with a hurdle [a frame of interlaced twigs] on their heads."[5]

One such evildoer was the Windeby bog girl, who was about fourteen years old when she died. Decay had claimed her chest and abdomen, but her delicate face and hands survived the peaty waters. The condition of her bones told scientists that she had lived a poor life and had not eaten in a very long time.

She lay beneath birch branches and a heavy stone, naked except for a woolen blindfold covering her eyes. Most surprising was her long hair, which had turned from its life-color blond to a deep peat red. It lay beside her, shaved off by whoever placed her in the bog. Though we may never know the reason for the young girl's death, it's clear her people believed she had done something terrible. Her punishment was a shaved head and burial in a boggy grave.[6]

Apparently the young girl found in Windeby bog had been punished for some crime.

Not everyone feared bog bodies. Some even profited from their discovery. One of the earliest instances of this took place in the late 1700s. Peat diggers discovered the body of a well-dressed woman in an Irish bog. Since the lady was so well dressed, the peasants took away her clothing, washed it, and then used it for themselves. A few pieces of the woman's costume were saved only by the interest of an amateur archaeologist, Countess Moira, who tracked down the dead woman's clothing and offered to buy it back from the peasants who had taken it.[7]

Another bog body, Rendswuhren man from Germany, made a tidy profit for a man who set the body on display in a cart in his barn. During the exhibition, visitors helped themselves to the bog man's clothing, and even a body part or two. Rendswuhren man, discovered in 1871, also has the distinction of being the first bog man to be photographed. His photographers propped him on his toes to take the picture.[8]

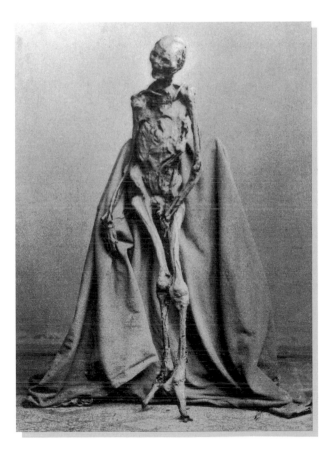

Rendswuhren man was found in a bog in Germany in 1871. He was the main attraction in a money-making exhibit.

Some local folk were happy to dig up a bog body every now and again, just for a peek. That was the case with the bodies of a man and woman who died from exposure one cold, snowy night. When villagers discovered the bodies, they buried them on the spot, which happened to be a bog. Twenty-eight years later, someone dug them up. They were in such good shape, villagers regularly unearthed them and reburied them for another twenty years. Eventually, the couple's grandson paid for their permanent burial in the town cemetery.[9]

AMERICAN BOG BODIES

Europe and Great Britain may yield the most bog bodies, but America claims a few of its own. In 1984 bulldozers unearthed the burial ground of an early prehistoric society near Titusville, Florida. Excavation stopped as scientists moved in to investigate the Windover site. There they found more than a hundred ancient graves of humans who had lived seven thousand to eight thousand years ago. Most of the corpses had been wrapped in grass mats and had then been covered with wood.

The Windover dig team (left) *worked carefully through layers of peat in search of bones and artifacts in the 7,000-year-old burial site. Archaeologists found two ancient skulls, each containing a preserved brain. A scientist* (right) *weighs one of the skulls.*

Archaeologists found grave goods buried with the bodies: wooden pestles, bone awls and needles, small hammers, spear throwers, and other tools. Their clothes, woven as tightly as today's T-shirts, surprised the archaeologists. They had always believed that prehistoric people didn't have the skills to create such finely woven garments.

Scientists discovered an added bonus. Some of the mummies' brain tissue had survived the long stay in the bog. Scientists were able to extract DNA from the tissue. They are using the DNA to get a better understanding of the genetic history of these prehistoric people who once roamed the land where Disney World now stands.[10]

ANIMALS IN THE BOG

Humans aren't the only bodies found in bogs. Skeletal evidence discovered in English and Irish bogs shows that giant elk wandered Great Britain long ago. Their antlers spanned more than twelve feet across, which means an elk weighed more than a ton. This is many times bigger than the moose—the largest living member of the deer family.[11]

In a bog called Burwell Fen in England, peat diggers found several human bog bodies. Close by, archaeologists discovered a remarkable number of animal skeletons in the bog: wild boars, beavers, otters, brown bears, wolves, deer, sea eagles, cranes, swans, ducks, and geese. They speculate that ancient people used the bog as an animal trap. The most spectacular find in this trap was the complete skeleton of an aurochs, an oxlike beast that is now extinct. Lodged in the aurochs's skull was a neolithic flint blade.[12]

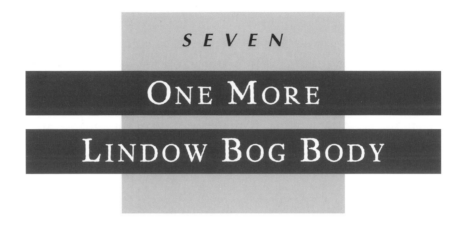

SEVEN

ONE MORE
LINDOW BOG BODY

If you think the Lindow bog story is over, think again. On February 6, 1987, peat-workers discovered part of the back and spine of another bog body. Rick Turner was again on the scene to investigate. Over the next few days, a search through heaps of peat piled on railroad wagons yielded more than seventy different pieces of a man's body. The only part missing was his head.

So who was *this* bog man? Scientists know that he was about twenty-two years old when his killers beheaded him. They know, too, that he died about the same time Lindow man did. Lindow III, as scientists named him, was less muscular than his older bog companion. His stomach contained the remnants of his last meal: bread and crushed hazelnuts. And as strange as it may seem, he had an extra, smaller thumb on each hand.

Scientist found no traces of clothing with his body, so it appears Lindow III went naked to his grave. But they found exciting evidence on his skin—traces of a blue, clay-based copper paint. The classical writers tell us Celtic warriors went into battle wearing nothing but a thin coating of blue paint. Until they discovered this body paint, scientists had no proof the Celts really had done this.

And what became of Lindow III's head? Forensic anthropologists can usually accurately identify the sex of a person by looking at his or her skull. There are times, though, when individual human differences throw them off the trail. Scientists are confident that the "dinosaur egg" bog skull, which they first believed belonged to Lindow woman, is really the skull of Lindow III. The two were found close to each other in the bog, and the carbon-dating tests show the same approximate dates for each.

While Lindow man's discovery generated excitement throughout the world, Lindow III has not, though in some ways he is even better preserved than Lindow man. For now, Lindow III's body parts rest in formaldehyde-filled jars in a storage room at the British Museum, waiting for the day when someone will complete the investigation into his life.

In 1987 another body was found in the same bog that held Lindow man. After carefully searching through the small railroad wagons holding the peat, scientists found more than seventy pieces of the body. Here they are carefully packing each piece of Lindow III, as he came to be called.

THE REST OF THE STORY

Four years after Lindow man was found, the missing pieces surfaced during peat operations in Lindow bog. On June 14, 1988, peatworkers discovered the bog man's buttocks and part of his left leg on the elevator belt. Three months later, an eagle-eyed digger driver spotted the man's right thigh and thighbone in his bucket. Only Lindow man's left foot has never been recovered.

When we look at the bog man, it's easy to picture him as he was two thousand years ago: a muscular, bearded young Celt. It makes us wonder about the man that once inhabited that body. On the day he died, did he wake up knowing that it would be his last day on earth? Was he nervous about the journey to the afterlife or excited about meeting the gods he had worshiped for so long? Did he look at the sky one more time before he closed his eyes as the ax was raised above his head?

And what of the people who were there to witness his death? Did his family and friends have a chance to say good-bye before he started his journey? Did they cry or rejoice at his passing?

Unfortunately, we'll never know these things. While archaeology and ancient history tell us a lot about people, they can never truly tell us the feelings that those people had. It's only when we meet a bog man, still clothed in flesh, that we can imagine him as somebody we may have known. His presence after so many years defies belief. Yet he, and others like him, are real, and their presence helps us recall that history is more than words in a book. History was lived by real people.[1]

It's easy to see why bogs face extinction. As the world population expands, we cover more bogs with dirt and housing developments. The United States and Canada will soon follow Ireland, Finland, and the former Soviet Union in burning peat for electrical generators. Germany, the Netherlands, Belgium, and Denmark have already used up most of their bogs, and our hunger for electricity guarantees that we'll use all ours, too.

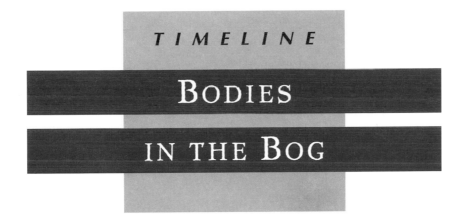

500 B.C. The name "Keltoi" (which would evolve to become the word *Celt*), appears in Greek texts. Greeks used the word *Keltoi* to refer to societies of people who lived to the north, on the fringes of the classical world. By the time of this first reference, Celts had spread over the Alpine region of Europe and to its north. They had also established themselves in central France and parts of Spain.

EARLY 50s B.C. Julius Caesar's successful conquest over the Celts in Gaul (France northern Italy, Belgium, and southern Netherlands)

55 B.C. Julius Caesar makes his first invasion into Celtic Britain.

54 B.C. Julius Caesar attempts a second invasion into Celtic Britain. Though the Romans were unable to establish imperial rule over Celtic Britain, there was considerable trade taking place between Rome and Britain in the years between this second invasion and final Roman control.

50 B.C. Tollund man and Grauballe man are sacrificed and buried in Danish bogs.

A.D. 43 Claudius begins invasions into Celtic Britain.

A.D. 50	Roman control is established over most of Celtic Britain.
A.D. 50 (APPROX.)	Lindow man is sacrificed and buried in Lindow bog.
A.D. 409	Roman imperial rule in Britain ceases.
5TH CENTURY	Saxons seize power and land in Celtic Britain. Over the next five centuries, Celtic British territories are assaulted by a variety of alien invaders: Saxons, Angles, the Irish Scotti, and the Scandinavian Vikings.
1773	Earliest written account of a bog body.
1781	Lady Moira buys back clothing from peasants who had taken it off a bog body.
1871	Rendswuhren man is discovered. First bog body to be photographed.
1948	Head of Osterby bog man is found, wearing hairdo called a Swabian knot.
1950	Tollund man's body is discovered in a Danish bog.
1952	Grauballe man's body is dug up from a Danish bog.
	Windeby girl's body is discovered in a northern German bog.
1983	Andy Mould finds "dinosaur egg" on peat elevator at Lindow bog. The dinosaur egg turns out to be a skull, first thought to be Mrs. Peter Reyn-Bardt, who was murdered by her husband. Later examination reveals the skull to be more than fifteen hundred years old and most likely that of the second Lindow bog man.
1984	Lindow man's upper body is discovered in Lindow bog in Cheshire, England.
	Bulldozer operators, preparing bogland for new condominiums near Titusville, Florida, unearth the burial ground of a prehistoric tribe.
1987	Pieces of Lindow III's body are discovered in Lindow bog.
1988	Remaining pieces of Lindow man are discovered in Lindow bog.

GLOSSARY

anthropologist   a person who specializes in the origins, physical developments and cultural developments of humans

archaeologist   a person who gathers knowledge about historic or prehistoric people by studying the artifacts, inscriptions, and monuments they left behind

aurochs   a wild ox, now extinct, that once roamed widely over the European continent

autopsy   an internal, surgical examination of the body after death, used to identify diseases or causes of death

bannock   a flat griddle cake made of oatmeal or barley meal

bard   an ancient Celtic poet

Belenos   a Celtic sun god

Beltain   a Celtic spring festival associated with the sun's warmth, fertility, and the sun god Belenos

boggan   one of the names given to the spirits believed by some people to walk boglands

C14   Carbon 14, a slightly radioactive substance that is absorbed by seawater and living things, and which slowly breaks down after the death of the living thing

carbon dating   measures the amount of C14 remaining in formerly living things; used to determine their age

Celts a group of people who once inhabited England, Ireland, Wales, Scotland, and Brittany

classical writers Romans and Greeks who chronicled the history of other cultures

computed axial tomography a computer-generated X-ray process that pictures the body's internal structures (abbreviated as CAT)

corpse a dead body

Diodorus Siculus an Italian who wrote forty books of world history between 60 and 30 B.C. (Diodorus of Sicily)

Druid priest of the ancient Celts

exhume to dig a dead body out of the earth

folklorist a person who collects the traditional beliefs, legends, and customs of a group of people

forensic anthropologist an anthropologist who studies the minute details of human skeletons

formaldehyde a chemical substance used as a preservative and disinfectant

garrote strangulation performed by inserting a stick into a neck noose and twisting it

humic acid the acid contained in soil and plants

hurdle a network of woven sticks and branches

keratin a protein made of strong fibers found in the outer layers of horn, hair, feathers, hooves, nails, claws, and bills

mortuary a place where dead bodies are stored

neolithic from the final stage of the Stone Age

Nobel Prize a yearly prize awarded for important work done in physics, chemistry, medicine, physiology, literature, and the promotion of peace; named after the Swedish philanthropist Alfred Nobel

pagan any person or group of persons who worships many gods, especially gods related to nature

pathologist a scientist who studies the nature, origin, and course of disease

peat bog an oxygen-poor wetland

pestle a tool used for pounding or grinding

phytoarchaeologist a scientist who studies the remains of ancient plants

Pliny a Roman naturalist and writer who lived circa A.D. 62–113.

postmortem   after death

prehistoric   the period before written history

radiologist   a person who analyzes and reads X-ray photographs

sacrifice   an offering of plant, animal, or human life to a god or gods

Samain   the most important festival of the Celtic year, celebrated on the eve and day of November 1

scanning electron microscope   a powerful microscope used to magnify objects many thousands of times their original size (abbreviated as SEM)

sphagnum moss   a soft moss usually found in bogs

Strabo   Greek geographer and historian who lived circa 63 B.C. to A.D. 21

supraorbital ridge   the bony ridge located above the eyes

Tacitus   Roman historian who lived circa A.D. 55–120

tannin   a plant substance used to tan hides

toga   a loose outer garment worn by citizens of ancient Rome

torc   a neck ring worn by Celtic people

whorl   one of the central ridges of a fingerprint, usually a complete circle

X-ray photograph   a photograph of internal structures made by using electromagnetic radiation

SOURCE NOTES

ONE: GRUESOME DISCOVERIES

1. Rick Turner, archaeologist, personal interview.

2. Don Brothwell, *The Bog Man and the Archaeology of People* (Cambridge: Harvard University Press, 1986), 11–12.

3. Sharon Beoley, "A Bare-Bones History Lesson," *Newsweek* (July 1, 1991): 66.

4. Brothwell, *Bog Man*, 11–12.

5. Rick Turner, "Lindow Man and Other British Bog Bodies," in M. Carver, ed., *In Search of Cult: Essays in Honour of Philip Rahtz* (Boydell & Brewer: University of York, 1993), 9–20.

6. *Science and Technology Illustrated*, vol. 5, Gruppo Editoriale Fabbri (Chicago: Encyclopaedia Britannica, 1984), 562–563.

7. Brothwell, *Bog Man*, 11–12; I. M. Stead, J. B. Bourke, and D. Brothwell, eds., *Lindow Man: The Body in the Bog* (New York: Cornell University Press, 1986), 144–161.

8. Charles W. Johnson, *Bogs of the Northeast* (Hanover, N.H.: University Press of New England, 1995), 35, 174–175.

9. Rick Turner, interview.

10. Ibid.

TWO: FORENSIC SCIENTISTS MEET ANCIENT HUMAN

1. Rick Turner, interview.

2. Ibid.

3. Stead et al., *Lindow Man*, 17.

4. Brothwell, *Bog Man*, 24–34.

5. *Science and Technology Illustrated*, 588–589.

6. Brothwell, *Bog Man*, 24–34.

THREE: DEAD MEN DO TELL TALES

1. John Dryden, *The Spanish Friar*, n.p., 1681, in *Bartlett's Familiar Quotations*, 16th ed. (Boston: Little Brown, 1992).

2. Brothwell, *Bog Man*, 34–47.

3. Peter V. Glob, *The Bog People* (New York: Cornell University Press, 1988, hardcover), 117–118.

4. Simon James, *The World of the Celts* (New York: Thames and Hudson, 1993), 64.

5. Brothwell, *Bog Man*, 35–37.

6. Ibid., 38–39.

7. Glob, *The Bog People*, 49–56.

8. Ibid.

9. Stead et al., *Lindow Man*, 140–142.

10. Ibid.

11. James, *Celts*, 95; Stead et al., *Lindow Man*, 167–168.

FOUR: WHO WAS LINDOW MAN?

1. Brothwell, *Bog Man*, 24–44.

2. Jane McIntosh, *The Practical Archaeologist: How We Know What We Know About the Past* (London: The Paul Press, Ltd., 1986).

3. James, *Celts*, 7.

4. Ibid.

5. Ibid.

6. Ibid.

7. Robert Wernick, "What Were Druids Like, and Was Lindow Man One?" *Smithsonian* (March 1988), 146–166; James, *Celts*, 7.

8. James, *Celts*, 95–97.

9. Brothwell, *Bog Man*, 95–96; Stead et al., *Lindow Man*, 167; James, *Celts*, 97.

FIVE: PRESERVING THE PAST

1. Wernick, "Druids," 146–166.

2. Ibid.; Stead et al., *Lindow Man*, 162–169.

3. Christina Hole, *British Folk Customs* (London: Hutchinson & Co., 1976), 212–214.

4. Stead et al., *Lindow Man*, 162–169.

5. Hole, *Customs*, 94–97.

6. Stead et al., *Lindow Man*, 170–176.

SIX: MORE BODIES IN THE BOG

1. Johnson, *Bogs*, 1–20; Stead et al., *Lindow Man*, 170–176.

2. Bryony Coles and John Coles, *People of the Wetlands: Bogs, Bodies and Lake-dwellers* (New York: Thames and Hudson, 1989), 173–197.

3. Glob, *The Bog People*, 66.

4. Ibid., 16.

5. Ibid., 153.

6. Ibid., 110–113.

7. Glob, *The Bog People*, 103.

8. Ibid., 107.

9. Turner, *Other Bodies*, 16.

10. Louise Levathes, "Mysteries of the Bog," *National Geographic* (March 1987): 395–397.

11. Lorus Milne and Margery Milne, *The Mystery of the Bog Forest* (New York: Dodd Mead, 1984).

12. Turner, *Other Bodies*, 9–20.

SEVEN : ONE MORE LINDOW BOG BODY

1. Turner, *Other Bodies*, 9–20; Turner, interview.

FURTHER READING

Beoley, Sharon. "A Bare-Bones History Lesson." *Newsweek* (July 1, 1991): 66.

Brothwell, Don. *The Bog Man and the Archaeology of People*. Cambridge: Harvard University Press, 1986.

Delaney, Frank. *Legends of the Celts*. New York: Sterling Publishing Co., 1991.

Glob, Peter V. *The Bog People*. New York: Cornell University Publishing Co., 1988.

Hodges, Margaret. *The Other World: Myths of the Celtic*. New York: Farrar, Straus, Giroux, 1973.

Levathes, Louise E. "Mysteries of the Bog." *National Geographic* (March 1987): 395–397.

McHargue, Georgess. *Mummies*. Philadelphia: Lippincott, 1972.

McIntosh, Jane. *The Practical Archaeologist: How We Know What We Know About the Past*. London: The Paul Press Ltd., 1986.

Milne, Lorus and Margery Milne. *The Mystery of the Bog Forest*. New York: Dodd Mead, 1984.

Place, Robin. *The Celts*. London: MacDonald Educational, 1977.

Reynolds, Peter J. *Life in the Iron Age*. Minneapolis: Lerner, 1979.

Science and Technology Illustrated. Vol. 5, Chicago: Encyclopaedia Britannica. Gruppo Editoriale Fabbri, 1983.

Simon, Seymour. *Hidden Worlds: Pictures of the Invisible*. New York: Morrow, 1983.

Wernick, Robert. "What Were Druids Like, and Was Lindow Man One?" *Smithsonian* (March 1988): 146–166.

I N D E X

A B O U T   T H E   A U T H O R

Janet Buell is an elementary school enrichment teacher. Her main interests are anthropology, archaeology, reading, soccer, and softball. The time she spent exploring a local bog made her want to find out more. In her research, she discovered the existence of bog bodies and other ancient humans. It soon turned into the idea for this book series.

Janet was born and raised in Illinois and now lives in Goffstown, New Hampshire.